The Love Tree

Poems From the Heart of Michigan

Richard Rensberry

Copyright © 2016 Richard Rensberry
All Rights Reserved

ISBN-978-1-940736-20-4

In accordance with the U.S. Copyright Act of 1976, the scanning, uploading, and electronic sharing of any part of this book without permission of the publisher constitute unlawful piracy and theft of the author's intellectual property. No part of this book may be reproduced or transmitted in any form or by any means, electronic or mechanical, including photocopying, recording or by any information storage and retrieval system, except excerpts used for reviews, without permission in writing from the publisher.

Cover Design by Richard Rensberry
Cover Art by Junai Meijer

Published by QuickTurtle Books LLC®

Published in the United States of America

Richard Rensberry

Dedication

This book is dedicated to
the boundless capacity
To Love

Richard Rensberry

Contents

1.	Invitation
3.	Farm Boy
5.	Tehquamenon Falls
7.	Autumn Fire
9&10.	Nebraska
11.	Lincoln Summit
13.	Critical Mass
15&16.	Blissful Spring
17.	Summer Love
19&20.	Harvest Moon
21.	Bride and Groom
23.	Do Not Disturb
25.	Honey Bee
27.	Embracing Silence
29.	Lost
31.	Bad Weather
33.	The Arsonist
35&36.	Epiphany
37&38.	On A Sunday
39-46.	Denied
47&48.	A Breath of You
49.	Carefree
51.	Taken
53&54.	The Coming
55.	The Going
57.	Insomnia
59.	The Yearning
61&62.	Where the Waves Break

63.	Morning Light
65&66.	Hunger
67.	Garden
69.	Heartwood
71.	Our Story
73.	Love Water
75.	Creation
77.	Without You
79.	Christmas
81.	The Lost Days
83.	Porcelain
85.	Hell
87.	Storm
89.	Thunder and Lightning
91.	Dinner on the Table
93.	Entwined
95.	880 Corridor
97.	Precious Beyond
99.	My Flower
101.	Hillock Hollow
103.	The Tree of Love
105&106.	Some Days
107.	Hugs
109&110.	The Dunes
111&112.	Keepsakes
113.	After
115.	About the Author
117&118	Pampered Beef
119.	Fairview Show
121.	Afterword

Richard Rensberry

Acknowledgements

Life's journey is side by side with others
and my life was not spent alone.
A special thanks to all who were and
always will be special.

Richard Rensberry

Invitation

May your heart sing like the mockingbird, lilting
bright as the monarch in the marigolds, red
as the blood of the Indian paintbrush
flourishing at the orchard gate, happy
as the pears and the Sweet-Dutch apple, purple
as the sunburnt plum.

May your feet dance like the breeze
through the copses of oak and maple, waltz
like the rain through the roses and rhumba
up the walk to our back porch, shuffle
to the susurrus of crickets and cicadas
'neath the stair where floorboards creak.

May the door open wide with a smile,
a hug, and an ice cold drink.

Richard Rensberry

Farm Boy

I chased the girls
from the Catholic side
of Thunder Bay. Two were pretty, freckled
and shy, but lacked the tears and make-up
about their eyes. Becky's were big, blue and direct,
speckled as eggs in a mockingbird's nest. Jane's
were brown, dark and deep
as pools of river near Ninth Street. Both
used God and humor
as their armor against me.

Richard Rensberry

Tahquamenon Falls

We slipped
out one night
when summer scents
filled the ditches
where the road dipped
through patchy fog. Our bike
was a whisper instead of a holler
and near Cheboygan, a mountain
lion leapt, missed or changed
its fickle mind. Fate, you said
had passed nearby, an omen
that we should live a little closer
to the edge of the risks
we take in our lives.

In Tahquamenon
you tumbled like the river
into my arms.

Richard Rensberry

Autumn Fire

We traveled that year
to Marquette
to raft the Laughing Whitefish.
As the leaves turned
from yellow to red
the north wind etched
a worried face.
Long silences
stretched between
all the things we didn't say.
On an awkward trek
to portage the falls, the tinder snap
spoke of ash
long before
the flames would catch.

Richard Rensberry

Nebraska

You had met someone, you said,
more practical and practically set
financially. I had my poems and ambitious bend,
you had your ends, so I raised my thumb
and hitched west to visit friends
near Pike's Peak. I pocketed and used
my older brother's Navy ID
to drink a few beers along the highway.

In Minnesota, I buried my head in a quaint resort
and painted cabins for room and board.
A week of fishing turned to a month
of depressing lyrics and tying knots
upon knots of macrame' hung in Brainerd shops.

In Nebraska, I bought a Kawasaki
and a pair of boots. I worked
part time on a small farm
and painted houses on Newcome Street
where I met a woman, more angry,

older, and betrayed than me. "Love," she said,
"rarely lets the heart forget,
but sex with me might do the trick."

It did.

Richard Rensberry

Lincoln Summit

When the road gets rough
and slaps you in the face
with bugs, fills
your lungs with dust
and the putrid taste
of diesel waste,
the romance ebbs.

Even a hot shower
can't rid the skin
of pesticides dumped
from crop dusters buzzing
the Nebraska cornfields.

We hankered and hunched
in the mountain air,
the storms that brewed
black and invigorating
as double espresso.

Richard Rensberry

Critical Mass

All atoms
from all suns
rain and ricochet
a nuclear storm—
there is no room
for a hapless finger
on the bomb. And yet
here I am
in a married woman's arms.

Richard Rensberry

Blissful Spring

If you care
to listen,
you might discern
hearts thrumming
beneath the bumble
of bees,
beneath the pink
and white
explosion of cherry
blossoms
that make us
tipsy
drunk.

So pungent
and sweet,
the petals swirl
in a blizzard and cling
to sun drenched hair,
to dappled arms

and freckled legs
picnicking
in nakedness.

Richard Rensberry

Summer Love

We clasped hands and slipped away
with the horses down the lane
into the meadow. Red-winged blackbirds
held chorus in the cattails
where the cattle drank. The creek had a rush
to compliment the laugh of the mallard ducks
and the air was abuzz with dragonflies.

I remember your face freckled and petite
as we knelt to pick orchids and kissed.
We snipped bouquets to freshen a nest
cradled in the limbs of an ancient tree; paradise
where we carved our names, then sunbathed
bare naked, satiated and carefree.

Richard Rensberry

Harvest Moon

I combed my fingers
through corn silk hair
picking watermelon
kisses
and the breeze
rippled
the deep pools
of liquid
flesh
intoxicating
as chardonnay.

The grapes hung
ripe
on the hills
and the valleys
sloped
into shimmering gold
cantaloupe plains.

Beneath
the pumpkin moon's
spell I feast
in a canyon sweet
oasis
of frangipani
and peppermint.

Richard Rensberry

Bride and Groom

In an ebon
glacial sea,
a lovely jellyfish
quivers and undulates
in ritual dance, billows
white veils
of intimate lace, propels
her red desire
up into the pale green fire
of icy light, flutters
and shakes, trembles
to embrace her mate
for that one
final descent
into the deep. . .

Richard Rensberry

Do Not Disturb

I am playing the harp
with a gathering wing.
I am jingling non-stop
a tambourine ring.
With rhythm and desire,
with fingers on fire,
I am writing a song.

On the edge of my breath,
like a whispering drum,
off the tip of my tongue:
a saxophone moan.
With passion and desire,
with my organ on fire,
I am writing a song.

Richard Rensberry

Honey Bee

His antennae
go whacko. He is buzzed
and rapt. His hairs stand
up on his toes as he twitches,
proboscis probing
for wafts of blossom scent.

You come to him
soft as a rose in the moonlight,
a blissful bud
that opens when you bend
knees and shed
panties of silk.

Richard Rensberry

Embracing Silence

In these vacant limbs
I know yearnings,
embracing silence
I hear many things.
You take more than yourself
when you leave;
packed within your suitcase
beside neatly folded jeans,
lies my box of joys,
my hopes, my dreams.

Richard Rensberry

Lost

I don't know where
to find desire,
once vivid as the color
of blood. I am lost
in a palette of white
with a bare brush.

Richard Rensberry

Bad Weather

The clouds are building
black towers, ominous
rumblings
somewhere intimate. I can feel it:
bare feet
on sharp rock. The lake's
waves rage,
capped white with foam. The barometer
has quickly dropped. The cold
is an ache
in head and heart, the rain
cutting wounds
once covered with scars. This is a bad one
in a bad boat
that weeps and leaks,
harsh as the crack of your mouth.

Richard Rensberry

The Arsonist

There is no answer
to the bitter things
to which we don't
consent. We seldom
reply to a whimper
or a scream, and what you feel
is never what
the other person wants to believe.
It's like a dream
where some forgotten secret
reared its head and woke
between us, something dire
at the precise moment
our marriage appeared
deep and complete. Then I turn
and there's nothing there
but the smoldering ash
of our neglect.

Richard Rensberry

Epiphany

The wind came screaming
down the road and jumped
on me ice cold
and brutally blunt
as divorce.

The land
stretched before me
was empty as a field
of white snow, fresh powder
on which to scribble
with angry feet.

I grit teeth,
stomp and pommel
with middle fingers
to the stars; laugh deliriously
until my spirit soars.

The wind

moans and flutters
against my cheek,
a little peck
like the nose of a cat,
purring.

Richard Rensberry

On A Sunday

Frostbite nips
the birch and maple,
yellow-orange and red,

as pumpkins blushed
sit stark naked
against the hedgerows.

Sumac flames
burn bright crimson
as a tanager's wing,

a cock pheasant
wobbles and struts
berry drunk.

The Congregation
sits dressed in their best
hats and gloves,

bob their heads
where pews creak
in psalm and prayer.

The preacher speaks
of vast abundance
as we slip out

behind the steeple
where snowflakes flutter,
manna from Heaven.

Richard Rensberry

Denied

1

We divided ourselves
and our wardrobes into different colors.
I was partial to cranberry and forest green,
she was more city, more concrete
in her grays and blacks. We didn't need lawyers
to define our differences as we spoke ourselves clear
of one another. We agreed
the world was bigger and more interesting
than our marriage. We parted as friends will part.

I was the demon that had to stand
before the Judge. She was ill tempered
with short hair and muscle.
She wanted to know what it was
that had led us away from promises
of love and affection. I explained
how sad we'd become—
We wanted to fold
our broken chairs

and get up and dance
one
more time.

2

"You must have threatened her," they accused,
"with a deadly weapon, or you beat her
with your fists, otherwise she'd be here
to defend herself. Is she embarrassed
or just too scared to show up with bruises?"

"What can I say?" I pled,
"She's somewhere in South Africa
sitting in a hut with a child
that needs her. She is smiling
and filled with peace and the courage it took
to walk away. She is happy and certain
she will get up and waltz in the glory of God."

"Thirty-two years," the Judge reprimands
and pounds her gavel, "has to count
for something. Divorce denied."

Richard Rensberry

3

Rachel had gotten rid of everything
she owned. Everything. She had no phone,
no forwarding address, no Facebook
or bank accounts. She willed herself a ghost
to dissipate into the mists of Africa.

Authorities, unfortunately, do not recognize
ghosts or anyone
without a body. Dead or alive,
it is required property. Voluntary absence
is much too hard to grasp
for officials in black. They get educated
in the belief that men are evil. I am ordered
by law
to confess and tell them— where
I had buried the body. "Arrest," they implied
"was imminent."

4

What was I to do? The papers
had been meticulous, the signatures

notarized and attested. I never dreamt I'd have to run
from a lesbian judge, but there I was
hunkered down
and seasick in the bowels of a container ship
bound for Cape Town.

I had my passport and two boxes
of ammo for my Beretta. I had told no one
of my plans; had left no trail of credit
or debit cards to betray me. That is the miracle
of ocean passage; of tobacco and whiskey
stained hands; cash whispers
and keeps you invisible until your feet fall
in a foreign land.

5

I remembered the name
of the village she had spoken,
it was Ha Lejone,
cradled in the far eastern mountains of Lesotho.
There, she had friends that ran a school
and I figured her rejoicing
atop the X on my map.

Richard Rensberry

I had to travel
two days and over fifteen hundred kilometers
to Johannesburg by train, another two days
and I was standing in the rain in Ladysmith
as close to Ha Lajone as I was going to get
on my own. I was a white face

in a black sea. The language was foreign:
a broken mix of Sesotho,
English and Funny. They laughed
when I spoke. I laughed back. We drank beer
and laughed some more. They stank

of cigarettes
and fermented sweat but were willing to guide me
over the mountains for a fee. The road they said
was filthy with bandits. Bad for a white man
to travel alone.

6

"We ride American horses," they proclaimed
and prodded me around
to the backside of their apartments—

a junk-yard, but with slightly less order.
There were several four-wheelers
up on blocks and parked
with their parts intermingled. They were crusted
with rust and a blanket of dust. They ushered me
to sit with a smile
as an engine labored for several cranks
then sputtered and barked reluctantly to life.

My driver was thin and attentive
as a cobra
with long spindly fingers and claw-like fingernails.
He had feet like a platypus and a mouth
chock-full of perfect white teeth. He grinned
and we leapt

7

into the bush of Africa.

8

Beauty is a story
with no beginning or end. It can take you
beyond your skin. It is more

Richard Rensberry

than the eyes can dream
or perceive. It is ingested and deciphered
like a breath of fresh air, it fills
the heart and the mind with poetry and warmth
enough to forget you are a fugitive. Africa

was beautiful. My guides
were fearless and alive,
uncomplicated with joy
and abandon. They had no past,
no future, it was now
into which I was swept. Trust

9

as a sense
is no different than taste
or smell. It is all encompassing
within the framework of living.
For some it is large. For some it is small
as if the persons themselves were blind
instead of the eyes. In America,
the authorities are sightless, not in the eyes
but in the whole. The judges
and officials fail to distinguish right from wrong,

gray from red, guilt from innocence.
Men lie, men cheat, they see it with their eyes
and believe it to be
a true and natural way of being. Trust
is a mistake. It can't be trusted.

But in the mountains of Africa
trust is worn like a coat. It is visible to the heart
visible to the soul like the words of a poem.

Richard Rensberry

A Breath Of You

When I take a breath of you
I am beside myself,
a place where lilacs bloom
and dew of clover
gives birth to fog
with purple fingers
reaching. . . .

When I take a breath of you
I find myself wading
through the north woods
moss underfoot
and waves of fern
like a green sea
beckoning. . . .

When I take a breath of you
I feel inflamed
sheets of lightning

and my being lit
is passionate and red
as Sumac
blazing. . . .

When I take a breath of you
I can't
    breathe. . . .

Richard Rensberry

Carefree

I want to lay in a field
where strawberries taste
like sunshine, where killdeers haste
a wing away out of reach.
I want to teach
our hearts to play
a game of clouds, kiss your
lips and tickle
your fantasies
as lark and whippoorwill hark
from their perch
atop a thistle. I want to whistle,
I want to hum— I want to bumble
along to a song
by Mumford and Sons
on a Sunday
or a Monday
with you.

Richard Rensberry

Taken

Listening
to the train
and the mockingbirds sing,
the cat is purring
like the murmur
of the rain.

I am taken
by the wind
sighing through the trees;
I am taken
by the blessings
and taken
by the ease.
I am taken
by your presence
in marriage with me.

I am taken, I am
taken.

Richard Rensberry

The Coming

I awaken to the echo
of my own heart
beating
like a door banging
over and over and over
on the backside of my head.
I look and feel
incomplete
as an empty cup
of coffee. I disentangle
my body from bed
to find longing has teeth
that gnaw in the chest.
I am bleeding.
The floor is wet
and scattered with red
rose petals, their skeletons
a vague memory
in a crystal vase upon the table.

I shower and shave and dress
and stand at the window. I watch
and wait for the sun and you
to rise.

Richard Rensberry

The Going

There's an essence
to the eggplant
that shares the color and curve
of your broadest smile,
your scent that erupts
from husking fresh
sweet corn, the potato
that stares
with somber eyes when dug
and pulled
reluctantly
from the earth.

Richard Rensberry

Insomnia

The tide is rising.
Too much moonshine
and firecrackers,
sirens and helicopters, thinking
of devils. A cat
in heat. A cat
on my chest. Thirst
for water, lime and tequila
on a Thursday with loneliness
wrapped around me instead
of you, my love,
instead of you.

Richard Rensberry

The Yearning

My being
empty as a bucket
rings
with something metallic
and impatient
as the skin
of a drum.

What the tongue says
doesn't matter
it is gibberish
to the ears
that want an answer
from the feet

'Andale mucho pronto!

Richard Rensberry

Where the Waves Break

You take me
Where the waves break,
Where the church bells toll,
Where the gulls squawk
And the thunder claps roll.

You take me
To the ship's stern,
To the storm's red eye,
To the dog's bark,
And the wind swept sky.

You take me
From the dark hour,
From the hammer's head,
From the cold sweats,
And the tempest's bed.

You take me
Like a fresh breath
With a twinkle eye,

With your chin up
And your softest sigh,
You take me
In.

Richard Rensberry

Morning Light

As the sun paints
wispy clouds pink
and purple, we wake to
dew on bare feet,
hints of lilac
perfume. Squirrels
rattle and shake,
chuckle and chase
among fruit-bearing trees.
A dog barks.
My cat's tail twitches
awake as fingers
and bodies perspire
like ripening plums
in the backyard
where neighbors squabble,
oblivious to it all.

Richard Rensberry

Hunger

Your fingers traverse
my arms,
tingle sensations
from rib to rib
and into my pants
as the oil sizzles
and snaps
in the pan. You ask

for knives and forks
with teeth all set
to dine, plates
with gaping mouths
and hungry plaints
for bacon, cheese,
and scrambled eggs.

I butter toast,
your intimate fingers
long flown off

to forage
among onions and peppers
in the kitchen sink.
I am left

sipping coffee and hopeful
your hands can remember
what the mind forgets.

Richard Rensberry

Garden

In your garden,
you are kneeling
among roses and tulips,
deft hands quick
as roosters snipping
petunias.

In your garden,
you are grinning
berry-stained
and tickled pink
as a snapdragon.

In your garden,
you are humming
captive as a bee
coaxing begonia
buds to bloom.

In your garden,
you are the flower
of my heart.

Richard Rensberry

Heartwood

We've grown,
limbs conjoined

and intertwined
like old trees,

inseparable
at the root

and coupled
at heart and trunk.

Richard Rensberry

Our Story

We are
like a story
with a rhythm for none
other than
ourselves.

Richard Rensberry

Love Water

I want
to be consumed
by blue pools
in wanton eyes,

slip my tongue
into the root of your smile,

lose myself
in the music and brine, enter
love's waters
and drown.

Richard Rensberry

Creation

I want to
conceive in you
a likeness of being
husband
and wife.

Richard Rensberry

Without You

There is silence and there is
    the silence of absence. Silence
that is silent has no weight.
It is brother or sister
to peace. It is the silence
of the rose or an ocean of poppies,
it is the substance of a dream
without bounds. It is infinite
trust for another. In the silence
of absence
I would be wanting
and scared. I would be
an echo
or a shadow made of stone. In silence
of absence I'd be cold
and alone.

Richard Rensberry

Christmas

Let sweet lips
fly like wings

and conjure a dream.
Let them scream

to traverse my skin.
Let them hunger,

let them feast,
let them whisper
flaming crimson

over me. . . .

Richard Rensberry

The Lost Days

We are casualties
of the season,
like onions and potatoes
sequestered in the damp
cellar recesses.
Instead of kisses
we sniffle at each other
and sit confined
to a cough and a sneeze, lethargic
as cats. Projects
sit dormant
and scattered
'til Spring.

Richard Rensberry

Porcelain

You stand
luminous
and naked
as porcelain, pondering
what
to wear.

I admire
and swear
I'd dress you
in kisses over
every square inch,
crack
and crevice.

You chatter
and choose
bluejeans.

Richard Rensberry

Hell

A moment
can be a hole
with a mound of earth
piled high
for our own
grave.
It can be a skull
full of spooks
or an emptiness
so vast
that all we can muster
is a scream.
It can seem
to have hands
that grab you,
feet that make you run,
or a heart so broken
and black
you can't see out. . . .
What have I done?

Richard Rensberry

Storm

We hold on
to one another
with octopus arms
and waltz
to the beach, whisper,
"I love you"
into each other's ear,
and later… strip
naked and bathe
in a barrel full of bourbon
and beer.

Richard Rensberry

Thunder and Lightning

The land grows
and roots our souls.
We flourish full
of sunflowers, thistles
and pigweed greens.

I am hard-headed
as winter wheat, you are delicate
as the flower of the artichoke. Together

we are thunder and lightning
making love.

Richard Rensberry

Dinner on the Table

I watch you tease the soup
with salt. Potato and leek
with a shot of juice
from a celery stalk. I can hear it
simmer, I can smell it steam
as you add your soul
like a cup of cream to the recipe.

It is food for thought
that love in an apron can seduce a man
to open his heart, and pang with hunger
as he watches you sneak
a habanero into the pot. But, if I had to choose
between soup or not, I'd set the table
with you on the bottom and me on the top.

Richard Rensberry

Entwined

Your beauty glows
rosebud rose
on a blustery day
in May
as crocuses uncloak
and birch buds burst
neon green. Your ardor
and passion for life
are free as the rapid
plunge into cadence
with me.

Richard Rensberry

880 Corridor

In California
I lose you
amidst the traffic
and commerce
of insanity.

Richard Rensberry

Precious Beyond

The depth to which I would go for you
cannot be measured or said in words.
I need you, yes, but it is less
than articulate when it comes to love
and trust. Those are precious beyond
and it is these things that bring joy
and tears to my eyes when you are absent
or lost in your search for peace of mind.
The first time we met, you wore blue shoes
and a wry smile, complete as your wealth
of beauty. I was struck by the certainty
of how you add your soul to mine. My search
was over. There was no one else or nothing new
in the world as bright and beautiful as you.

Richard Rensberry

My Flower

I love the unfurling
of the yellow rose,
the absolute beauty
in the stargazer's pose.

I love chrysanthemums
and the morning glory,
the way the begonia
unfolds its story.

I love petunias
and gold cowslips,
the way snapdragons
pucker their lips.

I love the boldness
of the lupine blue,
but my favorite flower
has the scent of you.

Richard Rensberry

Hillock Hollow

I want
to make love
in a hillock
hollow
where ferns unfurl
their curly toes.
I want to be swallowed
by sphagnum moss.
I want to be kissed
all buttery yellow,
sunshine naked,
gooseberry mellow.
I want to be lost
from the Internet search
gift wrapped
in paper birch.

Richard Rensberry

The Love Tree

You are my dance,
I am your feet
waltzing our smiles
that kiss and greet,

I am your sky,
you are my kite
flying our stars
in full daylight,

You are my bud,
I am your tree
bursting with Spring
for all to see.

Richard Rensberry

Some Days

Some days are empty,
some days are full.

Some days are timid,
some days are bold.

Some days are broken,
some days unfold.

Some days are some days
with no where to go.

Some days are precious,
some days grow old.

Some days are happy,
some days are cold.

Some days I tell you,
some days I'm told.

Each day I love you
is boundless spun gold.

Richard Rensberry

Hugs

You greet me
like a grebe
drying its wings.

I hold you
like a bee
wrestling
a dandelion.

We are
arms, legs,
and grins
in love.

Richard Rensberry

The Dunes

Our touch
is the gull
wing air

Our smile
is the sun
shine sky

Our laugh
is the wave
break song

Our kiss
is the sea
sand lips

Our sex
is the earth
quake shakes

Our life
is the joy
love makes.

Richard Rensberry

Keepsakes

So many joys,
so many tears,
time collected
in moments and years:

your favorite hat
you never wore,
me standing naked,
clothes on the floor,

the dog, the cat,
the goat and the sow
all in their moments
captured somehow.

Your sister Ruth,
your goofy brother,
your grandpa Frank,
father and mother

all in closets,
boxes and drawers,
shoved into corners
behind closed doors.

Richard Rensberry

After

Here after here
Gone after gone
Month after month
Dawn after dawn

Laugh after laugh
Tear after tear
Dusk after dusk
Year after year

Touch after touch
Sight after sight
More after more
Night after night

Kiss after kiss
Thrill after thrill
Time after time
I love you still. . . .

Richard Rensberry

Richard Rensberry is the author of Wolf Pack Moon—a book of poems written in January and February of 2015. It is available on Amazon. He is also the author of several children's books. His modern day fable How the Snake Got Its Tail and Colors Talk are also available on Amazon in both e-book and printed formats.

Richard is an award winning artist and writer from Fairview, Michigan. He is currently at work on his third book of verse and stories about the rural area in which he resides, called City Slicker's Guide to the Amish Country and will be released in the spring of 2017.

Richard is also at work on two children's books: A Boy and His Dream, a story about the Au Sable Railroad, and Goblin's Goop, a story about an evil factory and swarms of ambitious bugs who have a revolutionary answer to the Goblin's evil doings.

Richard Rensberry

Excerpts from City Slicker's Guide to the Amish Country:

Pampered Beef

Tom Trimmer looks out
across acres and acres
of pasture on loan
from God. He knows
the farm like the Earth will spin
long, long after
he's gone,
that his hands are guests
like the beef he owns.

They all have names
like Larry, Curly, and Moe,
Bugs Bunny and Big Dog.
Some are gentle
while others act mean
but all are pampered,
free range, and stress free

for lunch or supper
on local tables.

Crouched
on haunches
the carnivore prowls
like a beast in our genes, drooling
and whining
for a fresh steak
or a hamburger grilled
medium rare
somewhere in Mio, Lewiston,
or Comin's cuisine.

Richard Rensberry

Fairview Show

On the corner
of Weaver
and Cherry Hill Road,
Mary and I
spot a woodcock
drunk as a duck
walking
the gravel
shoulder of road
where quack grass grows
three feet tall. We halt
the Honda
to gawk, chuckle and laugh
as four chesty chicks
wobble wobble
out of the ditch
one after another in tow
with their beaks like pipers
doodling a tune
in a sister and brother show.

Richard Rensberry

Afterword

Relationships, like lifetimes, come and go, but love is a never ending flow of admiration and respect, physically, mentally and spiritually. To say that one could fall out of love with someone would be absurd, because it just isn't possible when love was brought into existence in the first place. True lovers only part ways with a greater reservoir of love to share with another.

Richard Rensberry

The End

Made in the USA
Charleston, SC
01 January 2017